PREFACE

The first modern edition of Monteverdi's *Orfeo* was Robert
that time at least fifteen others have joined the ranks of publish
or pseudo-scientific versions which, taken as a whole, make this opera by far the most frequently transcribed of all early dramatic scores.[1] No thoroughly critical and scholarly
transcription has so far appeared, but since the new complete edition of Monteverdi will
undoubtedly include one, the present score will confine itself fairly strictly to practical
matters. I am well aware that fashions in editing early music come and go, and I am no less
aware of the fact that the only excuse for yet another edition of *Orfeo* is that we may, barring unforeseen eventualities, come closer than ever before to the spirit as well as to the letter of the original. In the following pages I shall try to justify my retention of certain
hallowed editorial techniques and my invention of others.

The historical background

No masterpiece can be properly presented unless its interpreter knows intimately the
circumstances in which the work was conceived and first performed. In the case of *Orfeo*
the literature is not extensive, for the simple reason that remarkably little is known about
the details of that famous Mantuan premiere. The title-page of the printed score
(Amadino, Venice; 1609, 1615) provides only the expected bare essentials. To these the
libretto (Osanna, Mantua; 1607) adds one or two noteworthy facts: that the time was carnival time, 1607, and the audience was the Accademia degl'Invaghiti. In those days carnival festivities began on the Epiphany and ended on Shrove Tuesday, a period of just
over eight weeks. The young prince Francesco Gonzaga, dedicatee of the opera and a
luminary of the Accademia, wrote to his brother about a performance on February 24,[2]
which duly took place (as we know from a letter of Carlo Magni)[3] in the apartment oc-
cupied by the Duchess of Ferrara—Margherita, sister of Duke Vincenzo Gonzaga.

The actual room, just possibly the Galeria dei Fiumi, seems not to have been over-
spacious, for Magni held out little hope of gaining admission, even though he was a
respected courtier. But this peformance was definitely not the first, for Francesco makes it
clear that the opera had already been given before the Accademia, which was under no
compulsion to meet in the ducal palace. Indeed, the acoustics of certain rooms in the near-
by Palazzo del Te were infinitely superior, and concerts were frequently heard there.[4] The
real premiere, then, must have taken place between January 6 and February 23, most of
the soloists, chorus, and orchestra being drawn from local resources.

It is known that a gifted boy singer was imported from Florence especially for these
performances. His name was Giovanni Gualberto, and the prince praised him for
memorizing his part so well. The normal range of a treble voice would have enabled him
to sing the Spirit of Music, which not only dominates the Prologue, but surely calls for a
disembodied, spirit-like, choirboy sound. Euridice's virginal vocalises were entrusted to a
little priest ('pretino'), if we can believe a Florentine report of 1608, which also tells us
that he sang a solo from the safe haven of a triumphal car during Cosimo de' Medici's
wedding banquet.[5] Perhaps this mobile ecclesiastic was Padre Teodoro Bacchino, a well-

---

[1] See also *Monteverdis Orfeo: Facsimile des Erstdrucks der Musik*, with an Introduction by Adolf Sandberger (Augsburg, 1927). The article on Monteverdi in *MGG* (Vol. 9, Col. 528) wrongly states that
this facsimile is of the second edition, 1615.

[2] Domenico de'Paoli, *Claudio Monteverdi* (Milan, 1945), p.106.

[3] *Ibid.*, p.107.

[4] *Il Passaggio per Italia*, in which the academic Mannerist Federico Zuccaro gives a fascinating ac-
count of his visit to Mantua in carnival time, 1605. Brief extracts appear in Ademollo, *La bell'
Adriana* (Città di Castello, 1888), p.52.

[5] Solerti, *Musica, ballo e drammatica alla Corte Medicea dal 1600 al 1637* (Florence, 1905), p.55.

known Mantuan castrato who had been a member of the vocal quintet that went with Monteverdi on the Duke's Hungarian expedition of 1595.

Other members of this quintet may have taken part in *Orfeo*. Could the two bass singers Giovanni Battista Marinoni and Serafino Terzi have sung the roles of Pluto and Charon? Another probable member of the cast was Ippolito Fiorini of the ducal chapel of Santa Barbara, whose organist, Paolo Virchi, may well have played one of the keyboard continuo instruments. Ludovico Grossi da Viadana, then organist of the cathedral of SS. Pietro e Paolo, and on friendly terms with the Monteverdi family, could also have taken part. Other likely participants were the virtuoso lady singers invited by the Duke to grace and enliven the musical entertainments at court—La Sabina, Caterina, Martinelli, and Madama Europa (as she later came to be called), sister of the violinist Salomone Rossi Did he lead the orchestra, perhaps? Although we cannot be certain of this, it was surely the outstanding Neapolitan harpist, Lucrezia Urbana, who inspired and played the elaborate ritornelli for solo harp in the aria 'Possente spirto', for she had been engaged as a member of the musical staff as early as 1603.[6]

Editorial problems

Since the text of the libretto differs considerably from that of the score, and since no manuscript copies of poetry or music have survived, the composer's intentions and desires are sometimes less clear than one might wish. The errors in the score of 1609 do not always correspond to those of 1615.[7] Presumably Monteverdi, after trying out the opera first in private, then frequently in public, made cuts and changes (as composers are apt to do) on the advice of trusted friends or on the prompting of his own artistic conscience. The Mantuan performances were soon followed by others at Cremona, Milan, and Florence, so that improvements made expressly for these could have been incorporated into the edition of 1609.

Monteverdi was however no more accustomed to preparing operatic full scores for publication than Vincenti was used to printing them, and as it transpired there were precious few successors to this auspicious prototype. Inconsistencies and mistakes of all kinds abound, and while most of these can be tacitly corrected, there remains an ever-present danger of modern editorial emendation of the kind that has often wrought havoc with such bold harmonic spirits as Monteverdi and Purcell, smoothing down their expressive dissonances and tidying up their baroque flights of fancy so that they appear before us as very patterns of well-brushed respectability. When Monteverdi's harmony becomes problematic, I have had recourse to his own vocal harmonies as they appear in the works nearest to *Orfeo*: the Fifth Book of Madrigals (1603), the *Scherzi Musicali* (1607), and *Il Ballo delle Ingrate* (1608). The Artusi-Monteverdi controversy also yields precious clues; so too do the writings of Ercole Bottrigari and Giulio Cesare Monteverdi, the composer's brother. But the sum total of all this evidence points to the fact that when Monteverdi wrote something that looked odd or peculiar on paper, it usually came off well in performance, and he therefore is generally to be trusted even if at times his printer lets us down.

As the composer himself may have been responsible for drastically reducing the length of the opera, it seems pointless to cut it further. Several previous editions have omitted passages ranging from a few bars to an entire act, the former being as pointless as the latter is witless. No cuts have been made in the present edition, and none are recommended: the length of a performance should hardly exceed two hours.

[6] Ademollo, *op.cit.*, p.28.
[7] Some of the discrepancies are listed by Sandberger, *op.cit.*, p.(8).

Orchestra

Monteverdi's contributions to the art and science of orchestration, and in particular his orchestral requirements in *Orfeo*, have frequently been discussed in books and articles. He asks for certain instruments in a list printed at the beginning of the opera, but others appear as we turn the pages of the score, so that the complete array (in terms of an orchestral score as we now understand it) is as follows:

Woodwind:	2 descant recorders
	2 cornetti
Brass:	5 trumpets
	5 trombones
Strings:	2 violini piccoli
	4 violins
	4 violas
	2 cellos
	2 double-basses
Continuo:	2 harpsichords
	3 archlutes
	3 bass viols
	2 archcitterns
	2 positive organs
	1 regal } plural forms occur in the score,
	1 harp } possibly in error.

Since the purpose and function of this ensemble has been and frequently still is misunderstood, brief comments may prove helpful to conductors and instrumentalists. First and foremost, it should be understood that the apparent total of 42 would have been somewhat reduced because certain players were able to cope with more than one instrument. This time-honoured practice of doubling can still prove useful today.

Woodwind

The two recorders are called for specifically only in the ritornelli beginning at bar 91 in Act II, although their presence seems to be required elsewhere by the phrase 'tutti gli stromenti'. In the ritornelli the lowest note is treble C, so that descant recorders are perfectly suitable. In the chorus 'Lasciate i monti' (Act I, bars 73 and 182) only one recorder appears in the instrumentation, but I have suggested that both play since the two soprano parts move within approximately the same range and share the same musical motive, and the recorders simply double these parts at the higher octave. In other parts of the opera, treble rather than descant recorders are required because the range extends down to the F above middle C.

Although the old cornetti can be played successfully today, skilled exponents are few and far between, and in consequence these parts have been re-assigned to oboes. Needless to say, if you have the genuine article and the players to deal with them, the original sound will add a welcome touch of historical authenticity to the ensemble.

Brass

Monteverdi employs his trumpet quintet only in the fanfare-toccata at the beginning of the opera. In the Mantuan performances these parts would doubtless have been taken by the Duke's trumpeters, whose instruments would correspond to the five assorted sizes specified in the score (Clarino, Quinta, Alto e basso, Vulgano, Basso). But since heraldic trumpeters tend to be somewhat strident, Monteverdi directed them to use mutes, with the result that their music would sound a tone higher than written, that is in D instead of C. He also asked that the trumpets should be accompanied by the rest of the orchestra, and accordingly the desired transposition has been made in this score so that there will be a smooth change from the Toccata into the Prologue.

As with the trumpets, the five trombones would have been of different sizes in order to fit the range of the voices they are expected to double, for instance in the chorus 'Nulla impresa per uom' (Act III, bar 404). Since the five trumpets are used only once, and since five trombones may nowadays be considered something of a luxury, I offer the practical and (I trust) economic alternative of a brass quintet, consisting of two trumpets, two tenor trombones, and one bass trombone. This group can play all the parts allocated to brass instruments in the original.

Strings

The string section presents no problem except for the two 'violini piccoli alla francese'. This type of small violin, then in use by French dancing masters, was the so-called kit, or *pochette*, tuned an octave above the normal violin.[8] Unless museum specimens are available, it may be as well to play the brief passages concerned (Act II, bars 25-32, 41-46) at the higher octave, using ordinary violins. The thinner tone of the kit might be suggested by the use of mutes. It will be noticed that I have occasionally asked for muted strings in the ritornelli, since colour contrasts seem appropriate when (as in the Prologue) a short interlude is repeated several times.[9]

Continuo

The basis and backbone of the early orchestra was of course the continuo section, so that Monteverdi's list of requirements cannot be deemed in any way exceptional. Exact reproduction however is very difficult in our day and age, and most conductors will be content with finding reasonable equivalents in sound. A glance at the score will show that Monteverdi's orchestra does not provide a frame for the voices, as it does in operatic scores from Scarlatti and Lully onwards; its role is rather to alternate with the voices on the verse-ritornello pattern. Generally speaking, orchestra and voices combine only in the choruses. All the solos, duets and trios are accompanied by a single bass line, sparsely figured in the original, and this must be realized in two dimensions if we are to re-create the timbre and sonority of a baroque continuo section. First, the bass notes must be realized in order to provide harmonic support; second, they must be scored for continuo instruments, either isolated or in groups, so as to enhance each voice with the necessary dramatic or illustrative colours.

[8] Various incorrect accounts of this instrument appeared before David Boyden solved the problem in his article *Monteverdi's Violini piccoli alla francese and Viole da brazzo*, in *Annales Musicologiques*, VI (1958-63), p.387.

[9] Some idea of the late Renaissance attitude towards instrumental colour may be gathered from a document drawn up by Francisco Guerrero, in July 1586, for the chapter of Seville Cathedral: 'At *Salves*, one of the three verses that are played shall be on shawms, one on cornetts, and the other on recorders; because always hearing the same instrument annoys the listener.' (Cited in Robert Stevenson, *Spanish Cathedral Music in the Golden Age* (Berkeley and Los Angeles, 1961), p.167.

In a dozen places in the original score, Monteverdi states quite clearly which continuo instruments are needed, and it is obvious from these instructions that he had given much thought to the matter of weight and colour. Nevertheless he left large sections of the score completely free from hard-and-fast continuo instrumentation, presumably trusting the musical director to arrange for suitable changes from reed-organ to positive organ, cello to bass viol, harpsichord to lute, or whatever seemed most appropriate.[10]

It goes without saying that all the instruments except the viols would realize their harmonies and figurations with the sole aid of the bass and melody lines. Improvisation was the life and soul of performance in earlier times, and a modern production will best succeed if the continuo players will try to emulate this ancient and admirable lead by using my realization merely as a basis for further expansion. Naturally, a lute will provide chord-formations subtly different from those of a guitar, and similarly the kind of chord-spacing most effective on a harpsichord will not do at all for a postive organ or a regal. But these differences all make for sonority (as Berlioz pointed out in connection with parts for more than one harp), and they all afford variety, so that a run of several performances will offer no two that are exactly alike.

Depending on the availability of players, the continuo equivalents may be modified within a fairly wide range. I have recommended a minimum group consisting of arpa doppia (harp), cello, double-bass, guitar, harpsichord, lute, organ, regal, and viola da gamba (bass viol), these being signalled in the score by means of initials: A, C, D, G, H, L, O, R, and V. Each continuo player should use a copy of the score, entering when his initial is cued in the box below the bass line, and ceasing to play when another group takes over. The advantage of score over parts is that the conductor, should he wish to change the continuo scoring, can do so at once, without the need for re-arrangement or re-copying. Once again it must be emphasized that this is purely a practical solution to a very considerable problem.[11] If you have access to Monteverdi's complete continuo section, with two harpsichords, three archlutes, three bass viols, and so on, you will certainly enjoy making good use of them all. But few will be able to find one archlute, let alone three, so that the humble substitution of one lute, or of a guitar for two archcitterns, will count at least as a meaningful gesture towards baroque sonorities.

The lower strings of the archlutes and archcitterns provided, of course, a bass for the entire plucked-string section, and although this cannot be easily imitated today, the lower strings of the harp will be found useful by way of support. The reed organ, an essential ingredient in Charon's arioso, where Stygian gloom and a certain roughness of character have to be depicted, was in Monteverdi's time a small and compact instrument of limited compass. Its place can be effectively taken by a harmonium. The *organo di legno* or positive organ may prove harder to find, although the chamber organs built nowadays are sometimes small enough to fit into an orchestra pit. If a harmonium, for want of anything better, has to serve for both types of organ, it will be advisable to distinguish sharply between positive and regal by using higher or lower registers and stops of a markedly different timbre. The opening of Act V poses the greatest problem of all, for Monteverdi here asks for two organs and two archlutes, one pair being placed in the left-hand corner of the stage, and the other pair in the right. A possible modern substitute might be to place the organ and cello in one corner, and the lute and bass viol in the other.

---

[10]That a great deal depended on the acoustics and size of individual buildings is clear from Giovanni Battista Doni's remarks about the continuo instruments in his *Trattato della musica scenica* (c. 1635). See the extracts translated by Gloria Rose: *Agazzari and the Improvising Orchestra*, in *Journal of the American Musicological Society*, XVIII (1965), p.390.

[11]Other editors are welcome to make use of this system, with or without acknowledgement.

Basic realization

The few early 17th century examples of written-out keyboard accompaniments to vocal solos and ensembles (for instance Luzzaschi's *Madrigali per cantare et sonare*, Rome, 1601) give the impression that realizations at that time were by no means over-elaborate.[12] I have followed this course in my own realization, but I have not hesitated to bring in, when the libretto seems to demand such treatment, those typically Monteverdian dissonances with which his madrigals of the *second prattica* are permeated. There is clearly a place for diminished fourths and sevenths, as well as expressive suspensions, in a harmonic vocabulary such as this. But if my patches appear too purple here and there, I can only claim that when the opportunity presented itself, the libretto proved irresistible.

Notation

Modern key-signatures have been used whenever the tonality of a given section seems reasonably clear. When modal writing occurs (as in some of the choruses) the original key-signature has been retained. Time-signatures have also been aligned to present-day practice, and note-values have been halved in 'tripla' passages (Act I, bars 89-96, 197-204, 254-268, 292-306, 330-344; Act III, 153-159, 351-357; Act V, 138-144, 275-291). Many passages have been re-barred where the basic metre was obscured by the original barring. Examples of this include the Sinfonia at the beginning of Act II, with its courante-like melody in the second violin part, the Sinfonia at bar 397 of the same act, and the Sinfonia which frames 'Possente spirto' in Act III and recurs at bar 138 of Act V.

Every single recitative and arioso section has also been re-barred in accordance with the accents and declamation of the text. This causes a certain fluidity in the number of beats in any given bar, but in most cases the unit is of four or six crotchets. In my experience, it is all very well to tell singers that a barline does not necessarily mean an accent; a better solution, especially in monody, is to place a barline where a slight stress is called for by the natural flow of the text.

This principle has also been applied to some of the more homophonic of the choruses. The second section of 'Lasciate i monti' in Act I is given in the original (from which it has been slavishly copied countless times) with implied accents as follows: 'Qui MIri il sole voSTRE carole, più vaghe assai di quelLE.' Similarly in Act II, 'Ahi, caso acerBO' where a fluctuation between two-minim and three-minim bars yields better sense.

Although a double-bar serves as usual to mark the end of a section, the pause prolonging the final note of a cadence has in many cases been removed, so that the individual section will flow into each other and the unfolding of the drama suffer no impediment. In the Prologue, this practice has been carried a stage further, so that verses and ritornelli dovetail into one another, producing a real sense of continuity and integration. In the matter of tying bass notes over the barline, Monteverdi's printer has been improved upon, it is hoped, thanks to hints supplied by the musical and declamatory phrasing.

No tempo marks appear in the original, and dynamics occur only twice. Since these depend largely upon individual taste and choice, and rightly belong to that same spirit of improvisation whose importance has previously been stressed, they will be left to the discretion of the artists. The infinitely more delicate issue of ornamentation cannot, on the other hand, be left to chance. Monteverdi made it clear in 'Possente spirto' what he expected of a virtuoso, for he had the plain version printed above the ornamented one to pro-

[12] See the facsimile opposite p.709 (Vol. II) of Einstein's *The Italian Madrigal* (Princeton, 1949).

vide a choice as well as a means of comparison and instruction. It would be absurd, however, to perform an entire opera in which only one aria benefited from the melodic fioriture so obviously required at many other points and cadences. These would certainly have been supplied by Monteverdi's singers, for the fifteen years preceding *Orfeo* saw the publication of several important treatises on vocal ornamentation. Since these sources are not now familiar to singers, the appropriate cadential flourishes have been added in the present score.[13] Those who wish to know the original of any ornamented passage need only take the first note of the ornament and extend it until the next long note. For example, in the Prologue, bar 28, the original of the eight-note semiquaver figure is a minim D.[14]

With regard to the text of Alessandro Striggio, modern spelling and punctuation have been added throughout, and printing errors corrected. My translation deliberately aims at the literal rather than the literary, its avowed purpose being to provide a simple guide to those singers unfamiliar with the meaning of Italian, even though they may be able to sing the language perfectly.

Two textual matters demand brief attention at this stage, since they are closely associated with the musical form as well as with the unfolding of the story. In Act I, at the first appearance of 'Lasciate i monti', a double text is underlaid (in the original score) to the section in triple time. When the chorus is repeated, however, only the uppermost text is given ('Qui mire il sole'), which is clearly a printer's error, because there is no repeat-mark for the first chorus, and no opportunity therefore to hear the second set of words. These rightly belong, as the sense of the text shows, to the second appearance of the chorus, so that the scheme should work out as follows:

> 'Lasciate i monti'; 'Qui mire il sole'
> (Ritornello; Pastore; Orfeo, Euridice)
> 'Lasciate i monti'; 'Poi di bei fiori'

The other example occurs in Act V, at the end, when the chorus sings of Orpheus departing with Apollo to his heavenly abode. I feel that this final scene, from the duet of Orpheus and Apollo (bar 227) right to the end of the Moresca, should form a single and undivided entity. Once again Striggio has provided a second verse for the chorus, but it is rarely if ever used, although it provides a well-knit ritornello-verse structure which should be repeated *in toto*:

> Duet of Orpheus and Apollo
> Ritornello; 'Vanne Orfeo felice'
> Ritornello; 'Così va chi non s'arretra'
> Moresca

It remains to me to offer my sincere thanks to all those who have given so willingly of their time, assistance, or advice, and in particular Denis Arnold, Walter Emery, Kurt von Fischer, Nigel Fortune, Federico Ghisi, Jeremy Noble, Alec Robertson, John White, Desmond Ratcliffe and Michael Riches.

DENIS STEVENS
Columbia University
New York City

January 1967

---

[13] I have ornamented cadences rather than crucial words in the text on the advice of Francesco Rognoni Taeggio (*Selva di varii passaggi*, Milan, 1620), where singers are warned that such words deserve more subtle kinds of vocal expression than mere ornament. This *Avertimenti a' Cantanti* has been reprinted in Sartori: *Bibliografia della musica strumentale italiana* (Florence, 1952), p.263.

[14] Sources for these ornaments include the treatises by Girolamo dalla Casa, Giovanni Bassano, Giovanni Luca Conforto, and Giovanni Battista Bovicelli, all from the last two decades of the sixteenth century.

CAST IN ORDER OF SINGING

LA MUSICA (The Spirit of Music)	boy treble or soprano	$f'-e''$
PASTORE II (Second Shepherd)	tenor	$c\sharp-g'$
NINFA (Nymph)	soprano or contralto	$d'-e''$
PASTORE I (First Shepherd)	counter-tenor	$g-c''$
ORFEO (Orpheus)	tenor or baritone	$B-f'$
EURIDICE (Eurydice)	soprano or contralto	$d'-d''$
PASTORE III (Third Shepherd)	tenor	$c\sharp-f'$
PASTORE IV (Fourth Shepherd)	bass	$G-d'$
LA MESSAGGERA (The Messenger)	contralto	$c'-e''$
SPERANZA (Hope)	contralto	$c'-e''$
CARONTE (Charon)	bass	$F-b$
PROSERPINA (Proserpine)	soprano	$c'-f''$
PLUTONE (Pluto)	baritone	$A-a$
SPIRITO I (First Spirit)	tenor	$e-f'$
SPIRITO II (Second Spirit)	baritone	$d-d'$
SPIRITO III (Third Spirit)	baritone or bass	$c-a$
ECO (Echo)	tenor or baritone	$b-e'$
APOLLO (Apollo)	tenor or baritone	$d-e'$

ORCHESTRA

2 recorders (descants and trebles); 2 oboes; 2 trumpets in B flat; 2 tenor trombones; 1 bass trombone; 6 violins; 4 violas; 2 cellos; 2 double-basses; harpsichord; viola da gamba (basso); positive organ; reed organ (regal); lute; guitar; harp. Orchestral material is available on hire.

CHORUS

sopranos, contraltos, counter-tenors, tenors, baritones, basses

L'ORFEO
FAVOLA IN MUSICA

Edited by Denis Stevens

CLAUDIO MONTEVERDI

TOCCATA
(play three times before the curtain rises)

*These refer to continuo instruments: Arpa, Cello, Double-Bass, Guitar, Harpsichord, Lute, Organ, Viola da gamba. The Regal appears later.

attacca

PROLOGUE

3

From my beloved Permessus I come to you, renowned
heroes, blood royal of kings, of whom Fame relates glorious deeds
yet falls short of truth, because so lofty the theme.

19597

4

I am Music, who with sweet melody know how to calm

every troubled heart, and now with noble anger, now

with love can inflame the most frozen minds.

La Musica: Io, su ce-te-ra d'or, can-tan-do so - glio mor-tal o-rec-chio— lu-sin-gar tal - o - ra; e in que-sta gui - sa a l'ar-mo-nia so-no - ra de la li - ra del ciel più l'al - me in-vo-

, to a golden cittern singing, am accustomed

mortal hearing to charm sometimes, and in this

way to sonorous harmony of the heavenly lyre rather the soul inspire.

Hence to tell you of Orpheus a longing spurs me,

of Orpheus who attracted with his singing the beasts, and servant made of

Hades by his pleading, immortal glory of Pindus and of Helicon.

Now, as the tunes change, now gay, now sad, let there move

no bird among this foliage, nor let there be heard on these banks any wave

sounding, and let every breeze stop on its path.

19597

8

On this happy and auspicious day which marks
the end of the amorous sufferings of our demigod, let us sing,
shepherds, such sweet melodies, that worthy of Orpheus may be our
concerts. On this day becomes kind the soul once so
scornful of beautiful Eurydice. On this day happy is

10

Orpheus in her embrace, for her already so much through these woods
he has sighed and cried. And so on such a happy and auspicious
day which marks the end of the amorous sufferings of our demigod, let us sing, shepherds, such sweet melodies,
that worthy of Orpheus may be our concerts.

19597

Come, O Hymen, come then, and let your flaming torch

be like a rising sun that brings to these lovers cloudless days,

and far away now drives from them of sorrow and pain the horrors and ghosts.

Muses, honour of Parnassus, love of heaven, gentle
consolers of a weary heart, may your sounding citterns
rend from every cloud the dark veil; and while today propitious to our
Orpheus I invoke Hymen on well-tuned strings,
let your songs with ours be concordant.

19597

14

CORO DI NINFE E PASTORI

Descant
Recorder I S
Violin I SOLO

[Descant
Recorder II] S
Violin II SOLO

Violin III
SOLO A

Viola
SOLO T

Cello
SOLO B

La-scia-te i mon-ti, la-scia-te i fon - ti, nin - fe vez-

La - scia-te i mon-ti, la-scia-te i fon - ti,

nin - fe vez-

ADGHL

zo - se e lie - - - te,

nin - fe vez - zo - - - see lie - te,

zo - see lie - te, vez - zo-see lie - te,

nin - fe vez - zo-see lie - te,

nin - fe vez - zo - see lie - te,

Leave the hills, leave the fountains, nymphs

charming and happy.

19597

and in these fields to dances accustomed prettily the wanton

foot bestir.

Here let the sun gaze at your dances, more charming still than those

which to the moon on a dusky night the stars dance in heaven.

18

But you, sweet singer, if with your laments you once made sorrowful
these groves, why now, to the sound of the famous
cittern, do you not make to rejoice with you valleys and hills? Let the heart witness
some gladsome song inspired by Love.
Rose of the sky, life of the world, and noble offspring of him who

ontrols the universe, O sun who enfolds all and gazes at all from star-strewn

aths, say, when did you see a more joyful and lucky lover?

t was indeed happy, that day, my beloved, when first I saw you, and

.ore happy still the hour when I sighed for you, for then to my sighing

ou sighed; most happy the moment when your white

hand, pledge of pure devotion, you extended to me;

if I had as many hearts as eternal heaven has eyes, and such

foliage as have these pleasant hills in verdant May, all would be brimming

and overflowing with this joy which today makes me content.

I'll not tell what may be, in your rejoicing, Orpheus, that joy

of mine, for I have not within me my heart but that with you I stood

in the company of Love; ask then of it, if you wish to know

how much rapture it enjoys, and how much it loves you.

22

Leave the hills, leave the fountains, nymphs

charming and happy,

1959

nd in these fields to dances accustomed prettily the wanton

ot bestir.

Then with beautiful flowers by you adorn of these lovers

the tresses, that now from sufferings of their desire they enjoy blessings

215

215

Come, O Hymen, come then, and let your flaming torch

be like a rising sun that brings to these lovers cloudless days,

and far away now drives from them of sorrow and pain the horrors and ghosts.

PASTORE III

Ma se'il no-stro gio-ir dal ciel de - ri - va co-m'è dal ciel____ ciò che quag-giù s'in-

CGL

con - tra, giu-sto è ben che de - vo - ti gli of-friam in-cen-si e vo - ti.

Dun-que al tem-pio cia - scun ri-vol-ga i pas - si a ____ pre-gar lui____ ne la cui de - stra è il

mon - do che lun-ga - men-te il no-stro ben con - ser - vi.

But if our joy comes from heaven, as from heaven all that around us

appears, it is proper and good that devoutly to them we offer incense and prayers.

Therefore to the temple let each one turn his footsteps, to beg of him in whose hand

the world rests, that for a long time our well-being we may preserve.

Let nobody, a prey to despair, give himself up to sorrow, although

at times it assails him greatly,

so that our life is put in doubt.

32

As, after a stormcloud, its entrails laden

with black tempest, has frightened the world,

the sun displays more clearly

84

its shining beams.

36

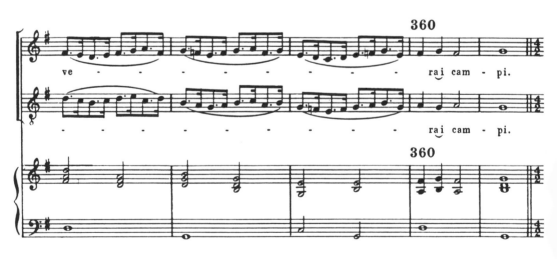

And after the bitter cold of winter bare

spring covers with flowers

the fields.

19597

CORO DI NINFE E PASTORI

Behold Orpheus, for whom only a short time ago sighs were food

and tears were drink, today is so happy

that there is nothing more that remains to be desired.

Act II

attacca

Behold, I return to you, dear woods and beloved shores by that
sun made blessed through whom alone my nights have day.

Look how it lengthens, Orpheus, the shadow of these beeches, now

that his scorching rays Phoebus from heaven shoots forth.

42

PASTORE III

Su quell' er-bo-se spon-de po - siam-ci e in va-ri

GLV

50

mo-di cia-scun sua vo-ce sno-di   al mor-mo-rio de l'on-de.

Violin I SOLO

Violin II SOLO

55

CGHL

60

On these mossy banks let us lie and in different

ways let each one his voice unloose to the murmur of the waves.

Pastore II 65
In que-sto pra-to a - dor - no o-gni sel-vag-gio nu-me so-

Pastore III
In que-sto pra-to a - dor - no o-gni sel-vag-gio nu-me so-

65

HL

70
ven-te ha per co - stu-me di far lie - to sog - gior-no.

ven-te ha per co - stu-me di far lie-to sog - gior-no.

70

CGHL

In this field adorned every woodland god

often has by custom made happy sojourn.

44

Qui Pan, dio de' pa - sto - ri,   s'u - dì tal-or do - len-te   ri -

Qui Pan, dio de' pa - sto - ri,   s'u - dì tal-or do - len-te   ri -

Here Pan, god of shepherds, was sometimes heard in sorrow

recalling softly his unfortunate loves.

Here the wood-nymphs

charming, a group ever garlanded, with

white fingers were seen plucking roses.

Therefore make worthy, Orpheus, with the sound of your lyre,

these fields where breathes a breeze of perfume from Sheba.

ORFEO

1 Vi ri - cor - da_o bo-schi om
2 Di-te_al - lor non vi sem -
3 Vis - si già me-sto e do -
4 Sol per te, bel - la Eu - ri -

CHL

1 Do you remember, O shady
2 Say then did I not
3 I lived then sad and
4 Only because of you, beautiful

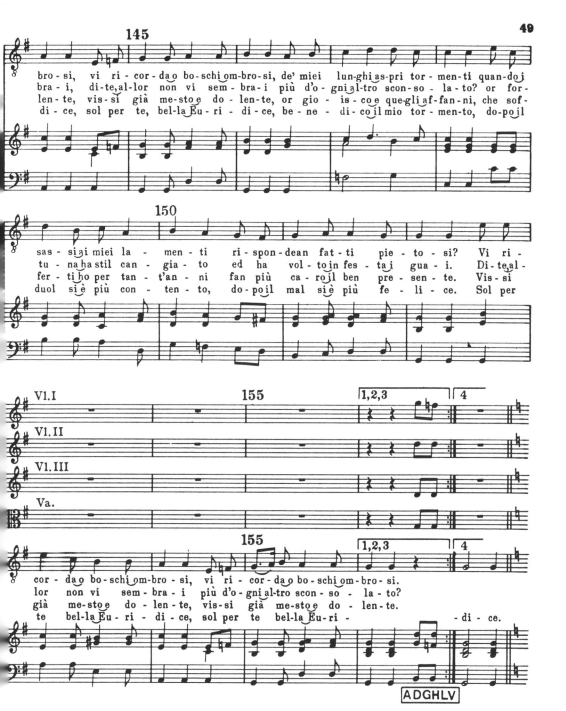

oods, my long and bitter torments when
em to you more than all others disconsolate? Now
orrowful, now I rejoice, and those sufferings which
uridice, do I bless my torment, after

e rocks to my laments replied, being made sympathetic?
rtune has changed her tune, and turned to joy the sorrows.
bore for so many years make more dear the good that is now.
dness there is more contentment, after bad times more happiness.

Marvel, O marvel, Orpheus, that on every side
laughs the wood and laughs the field. Continue then with
plectrum of gold to sweeten the air on such a blessed day.
Ah, bitter chance, ah, fate wicked and cruel,
ah, stars of ill omen, ah, heaven avaricious.

185

PASTORE III

Qual suon do-len-te il lie-to dì per-tur-ba?

CGH

MESSAGGERA

Las - sa, dun - que

GO

190

deb-b'i - o,___ men-tre Or-feo___ con sue no - - te il ciel con- so- la,

195

con le pa-ro - le mie pas-sar - - - - gli il co - - re.

PASTORE I 200

Que-sta è Sil - via gen - ti - le dol-cis-si-ma com-pa - gna del-la bell' Eu-ri-

AGV

What sound of sorrow disturbs the happy day? Alas then,

must I, while Orpheus with his notes soothes heaven,

with my words pierce his heart?

This is gentle Sylvia, sweetest companion of beautiful

52

Euridice: O how sorrowful her visage! What is happening?

Ah, great gods, do not turn from us your kindly glance.

Shepherd, leave your singing, for all our gaiety in

sorrow is turned. Whence come you?

Whither do you go? Nymph, what mean you? To you I come,

19597

Orpheus, miserable messenger of tidings yet more miserable and more

tragic. Your lovely Euridice— Alas, what do I hear?

Your beloved wife is dead. Woe is me.

In a flower-decked meadow, with her other companions

she was walking and gathering flowers to make a garland for her tresses;

when a treacherous snake which was in grass concealed, pierced her
foot with poisonous fang. And behold at once, colour
draining from her countenance, in her eyes grew dim those lights
which could outshine the sun. Then we, all downcast
and in tears, stood about her, trying to revive those spirits in

270

lei smar-ri - ti con l'on-da fre-sca e con pos-sen - ti car - mi, ma___ nul - la val - se ahi

las - sa, ch'el-lai lan-gui-di lu - mi al-quan - to a-pren - do e te chia-

275

man-do Or-fe - o, Or - fe - o Do-po un gra - ve so-spi - ro spi-rò fra que-ste

280

brac-cia; ed io ri-ma - si pie na il cor di pie - ta - de, e di spa-

285 PASTORE II 290

ven - - to. Ahi,— ca-so a-cer-bo, ahi, fa-t'em-pio e cru-de - le, ahi.

DHV

her lacking, with cool water and with powerful charms, but naught availed,
alas, for she her languid eyes somewhat opening, and calling
upon you, Orpheus, after a deep sigh, expired in these
arms; and I remained with heart full of pity and of
terror. Ah, bitter chance, ah, fate wicked and cruel, ah,

56

stars of ill omen, ah, heaven avaricious.
At this harsh news he seemed, unlucky man,
like a speechless rock so overcome by sadness that it cannot lament. Ah,
he would ceftainly have the heart of a tiger or a bear who did not feel for your ill
some pity, deprived of all your bliss, O wretched lover.

You are dead, my
life, and I breathe? You
have left me, never more
to return, and I remain? No, no, for if my songs
can do anything at all, I shall go confidently to the deepest abysses,

58

e in - - te-ne-ri-to il cor___ del re de l'om - bre, me-co trar-rot-ti

a ri-ve-der le stel - le, o se ciò ne-ghe-ram-mi em - pio de-sti - no,

ri-mar-rò te-co, in com-pa-gnia di mor - te. Ad-dio ter - ra,

ad-dio cie-lo, e so-le, ad-di- - - -o.

and having softened the heart of the king of shadows, with me I'll bring you back

to see again the stars, or if this is denied me by cruel destiny,

I will stay with you in the company of death. Farewell earth,

farewell heaven, and sun, farewell.

Ah, bitter chance, ah, fate wicked and cruel,

ah, stars of ill omen, ah, heaven avaricious.

60

Let not mortal man trust good, short-lived and

frail, which soon disappears, for often to a bold

ascent the precipice is near.

But I, who by this tongue have borne the blade which has bled

Orpheus' loving soul, hateful to the shepherds and the

nymphs, hateful to myself, where shall I hide? Bird of night

62

fau - sta, il so - le ___ fug - gi - rò sem - pre e in so - li - ta - rio

spe - co me - ne - rò vi - ta al ___ mio do - lor con - for - me.

Sinfonia

Violin I
*Trumpet I

Violin II
*Trumpet II

Violin III
*Trombone I

Viola
*Trombone II

Cello, Bass
*Trombone III

AGHLV

* These instruments join in when the Sinfonia is repeated.

ill-omened, the sun shall I flee always, and in a solitary

cave will lead a life to my sorrow suited.

Who can console us, alas? Or rather, who can grant

to our eyes a living fountain, so that they can weep

as they should on this sad

day, the happier it was,

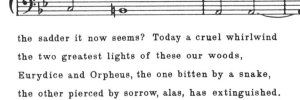

the sadder it now seems? Today a cruel whirlwind

the two greatest lights of these our woods,

Eurydice and Orpheus, the one bitten by a snake,

the other pierced by sorrow, alas, has extinguished.

CORO DI NINFE E PASTORI

Ah, bitter chance, ah, fate wicked and cruel,

ah, stars ill-omened, ah, heaven avaricious.

attacca

66

But where, ah where now are they, of the wretched nymph the fair and lifeless

limbs, where; for her worthy resting-place, did that sweet soul

choose, who today has left us in the flower of her youth?

Let us go, shepherds, let us go piously to

seek her, and with bitter tears let due tribute by

us be paid at least to that body drained of blood.

Coro di Ninfe e Pastori

attacca

Ah, bitter chance, ah, fate wicked and cruel,

ah, stars of ill omen, ah, heaven avaricious.

Act III

72

Guided by you, my goddess Hope, unique boon

to mortal afflictions, at last I am come

to these sad and shadowy regions where no ray of sunshine ever

penetrates. You, my companion and leader, on such strange and unknown

paths have guided my step weak and trembling,

and so today I still hope to see that blessed light which

only to those eyes of mine bring day.

Here is the black stream, here the boatman who bears the naked

spirits to the other shore, where Pluto has of shadows his vast domain.

Beyond that black pond, beyond that river, in those fields of

74

plaint and sorrow, cruel destiny
all your good hides from you. Now there is need of a stout heart and a fine song.
I to this point have led you, now further it is not allowed with you
to come, as a cruel law forbids it, a law inscribed with iron on hard rock
of the lowest kingdom, upon its ghastly threshold, which in these words

19597

the harsh order expresses: 'Abandon all hope, you
who enter. Abandon all hope,
you who enter.' Therefore, if you are still
resolved in your heart to set foot in the city sorrowful,
from you I go and return to my accustomed dwelling.

Where, ah where are you going, of my heart the only sweet

comfort? Since not far off now, of my long journey, is seen the

port. Why do you leave me, and abandon me, alas, at this dangerous pass? What

good now further advances me, if you desert me, sweetest Hope?

115 CARONTE

O tu___ ch'in-nan-zi mor - te a que - ste ri - ve te-me-ra - rio te'n

120

vie - ni ar-re - stai pas - si; sol-car que-st'on - de ad uom mor-tal non

125

das - si, nè può co 'mor-ti al-ber - go a-ver chi vi - ve. Che?

130

voi for - se ne-mi - co al mio Si - gno - re, Cer - be - ro

O you who before death to this shore rashly

come, stay your steps: furrowing these waves to mortal man

is forbidden, nor can he with the dead consort who lives. What,

do you wish perhaps, an enemy to my lord, Cerberus

78

135

trar___ da le tar-ta - ree por - te? O ra-pir bra - mi sua ca - ra con-sor - te,

d'im-pu-di - co de - si - re ac - ce - so il co - - re? Pon fre - no al fol-le ar-

DRV

140

dir, ch'en-tr'al mio le - gno non ac-cor-rò più mai cor-po - rea

145

sal - ma, sì de-gli an-ti-chi ol-trag - gi an-cor ne l'al - ma

150

ser - bo a - cer-ba me-mo - ria e giu-sto sde - gno.

to drag from the Tartarean gateway? Or do you wish to snatch his dear spouse,

with lewd desire your heart aflame? Restrain your foolish boldness,

for within my boat I shall receive no more fleshly

burden, so much of ancient outrages still in the soul

I harbour the bitter memory and righteous disdain.

19597

O powerful spirit

and awesome god

without whom

175

cui far pas - sag - - gio a l'al - - - - tra ri - va

_ far pas - sag - gio a _ l'al - - - - tra _ ri - va

175

al - - -

al - - - -

180

- - ma da cor - - po sciol - ta in -

ma da _____ cor - - po _____ sciol - ta in - van _____

180

to gain passage to the other shore

a soul from body freed in vain

live, no,

for since of life is deprived

my dear spouse, the heart is no more with me

and without heart how can it be

that I live?

To you (Eurydice)

I have turned my steps

through air

86

unseeing,

yet not to Hades, for wherever you are

is such beauty

as Paradise has itself.

Orpheus am I

who of Eurydice the footsteps

follow across these gloomy

sands where never

mortal man has trod. O of

my eyes, eyes lustrous, if one of your glances can restore me to

life, ah, who would deny solace for my suffering?

Only you, noble god, can give me aid,

nè te-mer dei,—che so-pra un' au - rea ce - tra sol di cor - de so-

a - vi—— ar-mo le di - ta con - tra cui ri-gi-

da al - ma in - van———— s'im - pe - tra.

and not fear gods who on a golden cittern only of sweet strings

arm the fingers, against which

an inflexible soul in vain hardens itself.

It flatters me more than a little, pleasing my heart, disconsolate
singer, your plaint and your song. But far, O far from this
bosom pity, of my strength an unworthy effect.
Ah, unlucky lover, to hope then is it not allowed that they hear my
prayers, the citizens of Avernus? Wherefore, like a wandering shade of an unburied

corpse, and forlorn, shall I be deprived of heaven and hell?

This much wishes wicked fate, that in this hour of death—from you, beloved,

far away—I call your name in vain, and praying and lamenting I wither

away. Give back to me my beloved, Tartarean gods!

95

He sleeps, and my cittern — if pity it cannot wring from that hardened

19597

He steps into the boat and crosses the river.

heart — at least (induces) sleep; fly from my song the eyes
cannot. Up then, why more delay? The time is right to reach the shore on the other
side; if there is none to deny it, let boldness prevail, since vain were the
prayers. It is a fleeting flower of time, Occasion, that must be plucked in
time. Meanwhile pour forth these eyes bitter

streams; give back to me my beloved, Tartarean gods.

395

CORO DI SPIRITI

Trumpet I A — Nul-la im-pre - sa per uom si ten-ta in-va - no, nul-la im-pre-

Trumpet II T — Nul-la im-pre - sa per uom si ten-ta in-va - no, nul-la im-pre-sa

Trombone I T — Nul-la im-pre - sa per uom si ten-ta in-va - no, nul-la im-pre-

Trombone II B — Nul-la im-pre - sa per uom si ten-ta in-va - no,

Trombone III B — Nul-la im-pre -

Nothing undertaken by man is attempted in vain

nor against him

more can nature arm herself. He of the insecure

plain has ploughed the wavy fields,

and scattered seed of his striving, whence golden

harvests he gathers. From hence, because memory

lived on his glory, Fame

to tell of him his tongue unlooses, that he

curbed the sea with a fragile boat, that

he scorns the south wind's

and the north wind's fury.

Act IV

My lord, this unhappy man, who through these broad domains of death
goes calling 'Eurydice', (this man) whom you have heard even a short while ago
so sweetly lamenting to himself, has stirred such pity
in my heart that once again I turn to offer prayers,
that your divinity to his plea may give way. Oh,

19597

if from these eyes some amorous sweetness you drew;

if it pleased you, the calm of this brow which you call your heaven,

by which you swear to me not to envy Jove his lot, I beg you,

I beg you by that fire with which already your great soul love has inflamed, make

Eurydice return to enjoy of those days which she used to spend, living, in festivity and in

can-to, e del mi - ser Or-feo con-so-l'al pian - to.

PLUTONE

Ben-chè se-ve-ro ed im-mu-ta-bil fa - to con-tra-sti-a-

DGHV

ma-ta spo-sa, i tuoi de - si - ri, pur nul-la o - mai si nie-ghi a tal bel-

tà, con-giun-ta a tan - ti prie - ghi. La sua ca-ra Eu-ri - di - ce con-tra

l'or-din fa-ta-le Or-feo ri-co - vri. Ma pria che trag-ga il piè — da que-sti a-

HV

song, and of wretched Orpheus let her comfort the weeping.

Although severe and unyielding Fate forbids,

dear spouse, your desires, yet nothing ever can be denied to such

beauty, joined with so many prayers. His dear Eurydice, contrary

to the fatal decree, let Orpheus recover. But before he stir his foot from these

abysses, let him not once turn toward her his eager eyes, for of loss
eternal to him is certain cause, a single glance. Thus do I ordain.
Now in my kingdom, make, O ministers, my will to be known far and wide,
so that Orpheus can hear it and Eurydice can hear it,
nor to change it is anyone allowed to hope.

O of the dwellers of the eternal shadows powerful king, law shall be your
word, for to seek other hidden causes of your will
our thoughts are not given. He will lead from this hideous
cave his spouse, if Orpheus will use his talent so that
youthful desire conquer him not, nor his serious orders scatter with forgetfulness.

112

What thanks can I give you, now that so noble a gift
you have granted to my prayers, courteous lord? Blessed be the day when first
I pleased you, blessed the plunder and the sweet deceit, since that for my good fortune,
I gained you while losing the sun.
Your words are gentle, of love the ancient wound they renew in my

19597

heart. And so let not your spirit be more fond of heavenly

delights that you abandon your marriage bed.

Pity, today, and Love

114

triumph in hell.

Here is the gentle singer who leads his bride to heaven supernal.

What honour shall be worthy of you, my all-powerful cittern,

if you have in the Tartarean realm been able to bend every obdurate mind.

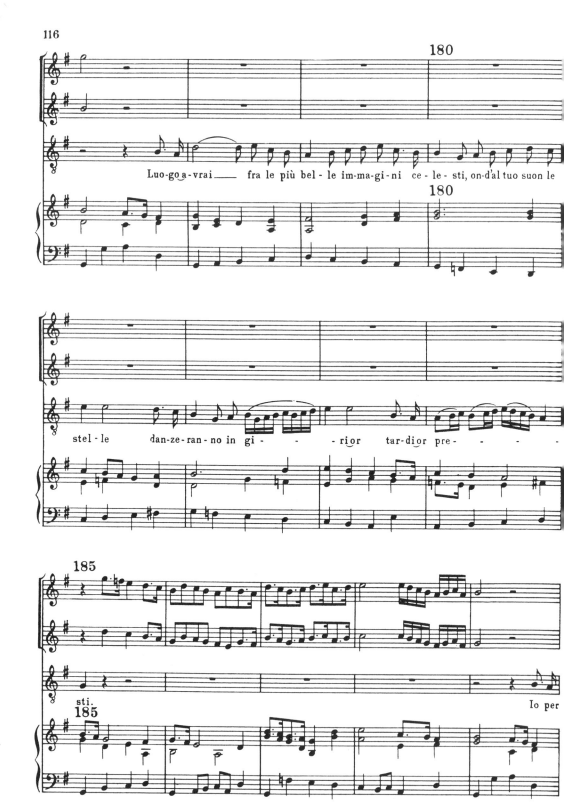

You shall have a place among the most beautiful heavenly images, whence to your sound the

stars will dance in circles, now slow now fast. I through

te___ fe-li-ce a pie-no ve-drò l'a-ma-to vol-to, e nel can — -di-do

se - no de la mia don-na og - gi sa-rò_____ rac-col-to. Ma men-tre io

can - to, oi - mè, chi m'as-si-cu-ra ch'el - la mi se-gua? Ohi-

- mè, chi mi na-scon-de de l'a - ma - te pu-pil-le il dol-ce lu - me?

For-se d'in-vi - dia pun - te le de - i - tà d'A-ver - no, per ch'io__ non sia quag-giù fe-li-ce ap-

you completely happy will see her beloved face, and into the white
bosom of my lady today shall I be received. But while I
sing, alas, who will assure me that she is following? Alas,
who hides from me of those beloved eyes the sweet light?
Perhaps by envy pierced, the gods of Hades— since I may not here below be happy

118

completely—withhold from me that gazing upon you, eyes blessed and joyous, which only with

a glance can make another happy? But what affrights you, my heart? That which

Pluto forbids, Love allows. To a god more

powerful, who conquers men and gods, I would do well to bend my will.

But what do I hear? O, alas. What if they, to my hurt, arm themselves with

19597

such frenzy, these Furies inflamed to snatch from me my dear one? And I consent?

O sweetest eyes, I can really see you, I still.... but what darkness,

alas, shrouds you? You have broken the law, and are of grace unworthy.

Ah, vision too sweet and too bitter,

so by too much love then do you lose me? And I,

120

245

250

255

wretched woman, lose the power any more to enjoy both light and

life, and I lose at the same time you, of all the most dear, my consort.

Return to the shadow of death, hapless Eurydice, nor further hope

to see again the stars, for from henceforth to your prayers will hell be deaf.

19597

Where go you, my life? Look, I follow you,

but who denies it me, alas? Dream or wild delusion? What hidden

power of these horrors, from these beloved shades

despite my will draw me and lead me to the hateful light?

19597

122

19597

285

Coro di Spiriti

285

DOHV

290

Virtue is a ray of heavenly

beauty, excellence

19597

of the soul, wherefore she alone can measure herself.

She of time's afflictions is not afraid, but rather

greater in man the years produce

his glory. Orpheus

conquered hell and was conquered

then by his own emotions. Worthy

19597

128

of eternal fame shall be only he

who will have victory over himself.

19597

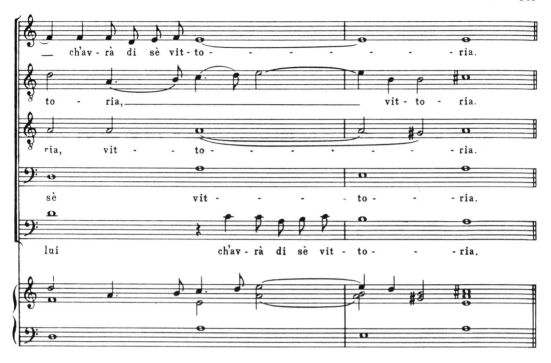

Act V

These are the plains of Thrace, and this the spot, where

pierced my heart, by the bitter tidings, my sorrow. Since

I have no more hope of regaining, by praying, weeping, and sighing,

my lost loved one, what can I do other than turn to you,

sweet woods, at one time comfort to my sufferings, while

it pleased heaven to make you through pity mourn with me,

to my mourning? You have been grieving, O mountains,

and you, rocks, weeping at the departing of our sun, and

I with you will lament evermore and give myself for ever, alas,

sorrow, alas, plaint. Thou hast wept! Courteous Echo

affectionate, you who are disconsolate, and wish to console me in my anguish,

although these two eyes of mine already through crying are made two fountains,
in so grievous a thing as my hard misfortune, I have no plaint such as
suffices. Enough! If I had the eyes of Argus, and should I pour forth
a sea of tears, the sorrow will not match so many woes. Alas!
If you have for my plight any pity, I thank you for your kindness. But

while I complain, alas, why do you answer me only with final accents?
Give back to me complete my laments. But you, soul
of mine, if ever should return your cold shadow to this friendly shore,
receive from me these last praises, for now sacred to you are my
cittern and my song, as to you already on the altar of

my heart a spirit aflame in sacrifice I offered.

You were beautiful and wise, and in you

heaven placed all her kindly graces, while to

all others of her gifts was sparing. Of every tongue all praises

to you are suited, for you hid in your fair body a soul more beautiful, as modest

as it was worthy of honour. Now other women are
proud and deceitful towards men who adore them, unpitying and
untrustful, devoid of sense and of every noble thought, wherefore by
reason their deeds cannot be praised, and it will never be that through vile
woman, Love with golden arrow shall pierce my heart.

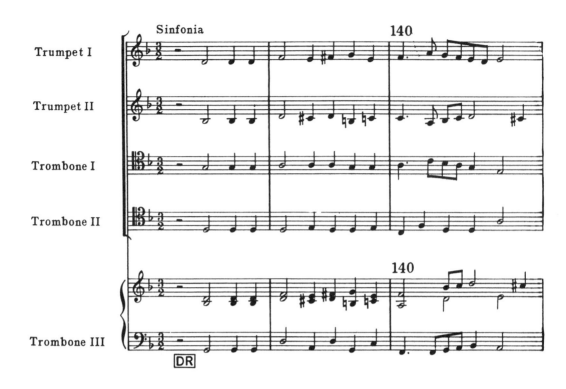

Apollo descends, singing, in a cloud

145 APOLLO

Per-chè a lo sde-gno e al do-lor in pre-da co - sì ti do - nio fi - glio? Non è, non è con-si-glio di ge-ne-ro - so pet - to ser - vir al pro-prio af - fet - to. Quin - ci bias-mo e pe - ri-glio già so-vra-star ti veg - gio, on-de mo - vo dal ciel per dar ti a - i - ta. Or tu m'a - scol - ta e

AGHV

Why to scorn and sorrow a prey, do you so give yourself, O son?

It is not wisdom, in a generous heart, to

be a slave to one's own emotions. Since blame and peril

already I see you overpower, for this reason I come from heaven to give you

help. Now you listen to me and

of it you shall have praise and life. Gracious father, in time of greatest need

you come, for to a desperate end and with extreme grief

they have led me, scorn and love. Here I am then

attentive to your commands celestial father, now whatever you wish, command me.

Too much you enjoyed your happy lot, now too much

you lament your fate, bitter and harsh. Still know you not how no
earthly pleasure is lasting? Therefore if you desire to enjoy immortal
life, come with me to heaven, which to itself invites you.
So, shall I no more see of dear Eurydice the sweet
eyes? In the sun and in the stars you will view with delight

her lovely semblance. Indeed of such a father I would not be

a worthy son, if I did not follow your faithful counsel.

Let us rise

singing

to heaven, where true virtue

has its own reward, joy and peace.

260

260

attacca

CORO DI NINFE E PASTORI

Violin I S

Van-ne Or-feo fe - li-ce a pie - no,
Co - si va chi non s'ar - re - tra

Violin II S

Van-ne Or-feo fe - li - ce a pie - no, a go -
Co - si va chi non s'ar - re - tra al chia -

Violin III A

Van-ne Or-feo fe - li - ce a pie - no, a go -
Co - si va chi non s'ar - re - tra al chia -

Viola T

Van-ne Or-feo, van-ne Or-feo fe - li-ce a pie - no, a go -
Co - si va, co - si va chi non s'ar - re - tra al chia -

Cello B

Van-ne Or-feo fe - li - ce a pie - no, a go -
Co - si va chi non s'ar - re - tra al chia -

Bass

AHLO

Go. Orpheus, utterly happy

Thus goes he who does not resist

146

to enjoy heavenly honours, there where goodness is never

to the calling of an everlasting god, thus does he grace in heaven

diminished, there where never sorrow was, while

obtain who here below has braved hell. And whoever

altars, incense, and vows we offer you, happy and devout.

ows in sorrow, of every grace the fruit reaps.

148

Printed and bound in Great Britain by
Caligraving Limited Thetford Norfolk

CRITICAL NOTES

Page 14/bar 79: The part-writing in alto and tenor voices is retained at the repeat (22/187) where the reading of the original is less satisfactory.

30/260: Third violin has a semibreve followed by a minim rest, presumably to allow the player to lift and replace his bow. I have sustained the note here and in the subsequent repeats of this ritornello.

36/347-48: The harsh frosts of winter appear in the original second tenor part as C C A♯, but the C naturals are unlikely here since the ostinato calls for an A major chord (cf.31/271 and 33/309). On the other hand, the augmented triad at the word 'gel' is not beyond the bounds of possibility, bearing in mind Monteverdi's expressive use of this chord in his early books of madrigals.

36/353-4: Since the dotted rhythm permeates this verse, I have continued it in these two bars, as it was almost certainly so intended to be sung.

45/94: The original bass gives a dotted minim and crotchet, but I have inserted the octave leap to aid the rhythmic flow. Similar minor changes occur later in this section.

54/252: No ♯ to 'piè'. It is just possible that a chromatic change from G to G♯ was prompted by the image of a poisonous snake.

83/200: The ornamented part has the notes A F above 'nonè'.

85/217: The solo line suggests D major just as cogently as the harp part suggests D minor. Previous statements of the ostinato (80/164-7; 83/192-5) show that the chord tends to fluctuate, so I have made the soloist's semibreve into a minim and changed the chord at the middle of the bar.

87/233: The five-note figure beginning at the syllable 'di' is usually transcribed in notes double the length, as the original is unclear at this point due to broken type.

87/238: The second half of the bar, treble stave, appears a tone higher in the original, and has been emended here by analogy with 88/240-1.

88/241: The four-note group (third beat, treble stave) appears a third lower in the original, but the placing of a flat before the second note shows that F, was meant, and not C.

111/109: D minim originally semibreve.

111/115: The notes above 'nè i gravi' originally double length.

MONTEVERDI'S NOTES ON ORCHESTRATION

1/1: Toccata che si suona avanti il levar de la tela tre volte con tutti li stromenti, et si fa un Tuono più alto volendo sonar le trombe con le sordine.

11/37: Questo Canto fu concertato al suono de tutti gli stromenti.

14/73: Questo Balletto fu cantato al suono di cinque Viole da braccio, tre Chittaroni, duoi Clavicembani, un'Arpa doppia, un contrabasso de Viola, et un Flautino alla vigesima seconda.

40/25: Questo Ritornello fu sonato di dentro da un Clavicembano, duoi Chitaroni, at duoi Violini piccioli alla Francese.

42/54: Questo Ritornello fu suonato da duoi Violini ordinarij da braccio, un Basso de Viola da braccio, un Clavicembano, et duoi Chittaroni.

43/64: Un Clavicembano et un Chittarone.

45/91: Fu suonato di dentro da Chitaroni un Clavicebano et duoi Flautini.

47/134: Fu suonato questo Ritornello di dentro da cinque Viole da braccio, un contrabasso, duoi Clavicembani et tre chitarroni.

50/172: Un organo di legno et un Chit.

51/183: Un Clavic. Chitar. & Viola da bracio.

57/312: Un organo di legno et un Chitarone.

63/406: Duoi Pastori cantano al suono del Organo di legno, et un Chittarone.

70/1: Qui entrano li Tromb. Corn. & Regali, & taciono le Viole da bracio, & Organi di legno Clavacem. & si muta la Sena.

77/115: Caronte canta al suono del Regale.

80/160: Orfeo al suono del Organo di legno, & un Chitarrone, canta una sola de le due parti. Violino/Violino.

83/192: Duoi Cornetti.

85/217: Arpa doppia (repeated in smaller type below bass stave).

89/253: 2 Violini, Basso da brazzo.

91/290: Furono sonate le altre parti da tre Viole da braccio, & un contrabasso de Viola tocchi pian piano.

95/351: Questa Sinfo. si sonò pian piano, con Viole da braccio, un Org. di leg. & un contrabasso de Viola da gamba.

95/358: Orfeo canta al suono del Organo di legno solamente.

96/380: Qui entra nella barca e passa cantando al suono del Organo di legno.

99/404: Coro de spirti, al suono di un Reg. Org. di legno, cinque Tromb. duoi Bassi da gamba, & un contrabasso de viola.

114/161: Violino/Violino.

118/219: Segue Orfeo cantando nel Clavicembano Viola da braccio. & Chittarone.

119/225: Qui si volta Orfeo. & canta al suono del Organo di legno.

119/230: Qui canta Orfeo al suono del Clavic. Viola da braccio basso, & un chitar.

131/1: Tacciono li Cornetti, Tromboni & Regali, & entrano a sonare il presente Ritornello, le viole da braccio, Organi Clavicembani, contrabasso, & Arpe, & Chitaroni, & Ceteroni, & si muta la Sena.

131/9: Duoi Organi di legno. & duoi Chitaroni concertono questo Canto sonando l'uno nel angolo sinistro de la Sena, l'altro nel destro.

CHORAL WORKS
FOR MIXED VOICES

Bach   **Christmas Oratorio**
for soprano, alto, tenor & bass soli, SATB & orchestra

Mass in B minor
for two sopranos, alto, tenor & bass soli, SSATB & orchestra

St Matthew Passion
for soprano, alto, tenor & bass soli, SATB & orchestra

Brahms   **Requiem**
for soprano & baritone soli, SATB & orchestra

Elgar   **Give unto the Lord**   **Psalm 29**
for SATB & organ or orchestra

Fauré   **Requiem**
for soprano & baritone soli, SATB & orchestra
edited by Desmond Ratcliffe

Handel   **Messiah**
for soprano, alto, tenor & bass soli, SATB & orchestra
edited by Watkins Shaw

Haydn   **Creation**
for soprano, tenor & bass soli, SATB & orchestra

Imperial 'Nelson' Mass
for soprano, alto, tenor & bass soli, SATB & orchestra

Maria Theresa Mass
for soprano, alto, tenor & bass soli, SATB & orchestra

Mass in time of War 'Paukenmesse'
for soprano, alto, tenor & bass soli, SATB & orchestra

Monteverdi   **Beatus Vir**
for soloists, double choir, organ & orchestra
edited by Denis Stevens & John Steele

Magnificat
for SSATB chorus, instruments & organ
edited by John Steele

Vespers
for soloists, double choir, organ & orchestra
edited by Denis Stevens

Mozart   **Requiem Mass**
for soprano, alto, tenor & bass soli, SATB & orchestra

Scarlatti   **Dixit Dominus**
for SATB, soli & chorus, string orchestra & organ continuo
edited by John Steele

901(83)